VERONICA MARECLE

FINDING JESUS in Christmas

a Seek and Find for all ages

ILLUSTRATIONS BY J D DAVENPORT

Finding Jesus in Christmas

ISBN 979-8-9887414-0-4

Alll Scripture taken from the KING JAMES VERSION.

First printing 2023

Printed in USA

For those who planted seeds, those who came along and watered them, and for the One who found something in me redeemable, and to my husband, my mom, my supportive family and friends, may the greatest Story ever told captivate our hearts again — Veronica

In memory of my mother, Betty J. Davenport, and with love and gratitude to my wife, Rita G. Davenport, both of who inspired me to follow Christ and to pursue my dreams— JD

For unto us a child is born, unto us a son is given: and the government shall be upon his shoulder: and his name shall be called Wonderful, Counsellor, The mighty God, The everlasting Father, The Prince of Peace.

Isaiah 9:6

PREFACE

Busy, distracted, chaotic— it's the culture in which we live. Add the holiday season to our already overcommitted agendas, and keeping Christ at the center is an almost impossible feat regardless of all of our good intentions. I imagine the town of Bethlehem during the census was much like our modern-day Black Friday and Christmas shopping season. Crowded pandemonium is likely a better description than the Silent Night of which we've all sung. It's no wonder the people in Bethlehem were too distracted to hear the hosts of angels singing nearby or see the new star appear that night. Let's face it, if the Messiah made His debut in the middle of our madness, we would likely miss all the clues too.

So how do we prepare our hearts during this incredibly busy season of Advent? How do we keep Christ at the center and the focus of our daily life, especially during the holidays?

A few years ago, after speaking at a Christmas tea and sharing my comparison of the census season to our busy Christmas season, my sister-in-law Lori challenged me to put my words into print. "Make it a seek-and-find," she said.

That season of Christmas was one of the busiest ever, but I accepted Lori's challenge and spent the following two weeks seeking and finding Jesus amid our holiday hustle and bustle, and I found Him! I found Him in some of the most unlikely places.

And, now, I'm passing along this challenge to you! Seek the Lord, and you will find Him too! Make this a new tradition with your family, and it will transform your season of advent.

This isn't a traditional seek-and-find book, not an activity book you can read once and memorize where all the hidden images are located. Instead, each time you open this book, JD and I hope you will find a new image of Jesus; and we hope that even after you've closed the book, you will learn to seek Him as you're running your errands, completing your to-do lists, attending those parties, and baking those goodies. Engage your children and families in searching for Jesus too!

May your search uncover the Prince of Peace, the Lamb of God, the Everlasting Father, the Light of the World, the Tree of Life, and the Bright Morning Star. May you find the Provider within His provision, the Gift, as well as, the Giver, the Joy of the world, the Hope for all generations, the Promise, and the Promise-Keeper. And in your finding, may you experience His abundant grace, His never-ending mercy, and His unconditional love.

After all, He is Emanuel, God with us. He isn't hiding! He's all around us! He goes before us, walks beside us, follows behind us, and dwells within us!

Seek Him, and you will find Him! Matthew 7:7

And ye shall seek me, and find me, when ye shall search for me with all your heart.

Jeremiah 29:13

It was time for the census in Bethlehem town,

Each family in the region came from miles all around.

More and more travelers were arriving each day;

So many had come, there was no room to stay.

Crowded and busy, the city was packed.

There to register for the census and pay all their tax.

Trading their crafts for the items they need,

There were cattle and blankets and every kind of seed.

Visiting family and friends while they were in town,
It had been such a long time since they were around.

At least a year it would be before traveling back this way,
They were doing as much as they possibly could each day.

So busy were the town's people and visitors too,

They didn't notice young Mary with a baby soon due.

No place to stay, as they knocked on each door.

There wasn't even room for a pallet on the floor.

Finally, an inn keeper offered a space out back.

There'd be no bed, no breakfast, and a bath it would lack.

In a stable filled with animals and yucky smells too,

Young Mary and Joseph unpacked their mule.

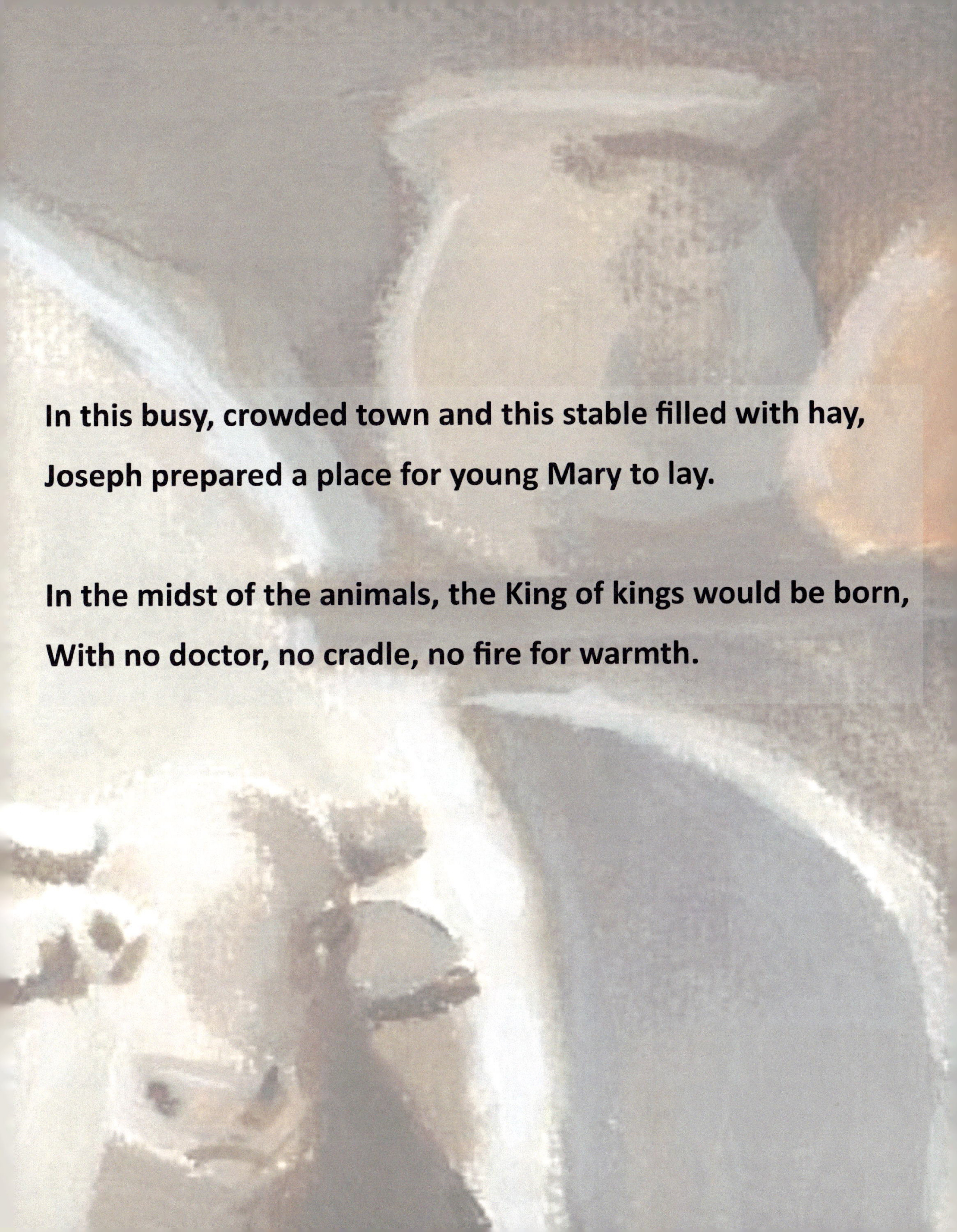

In this busy, crowded town and this stable filled with hay,

Joseph prepared a place for young Mary to lay.

In the midst of the animals, the King of kings would be born,

With no doctor, no cradle, no fire for warmth.

That's where sweet Jesus made His debut,

Yet, all the people in the town missed all the clues!

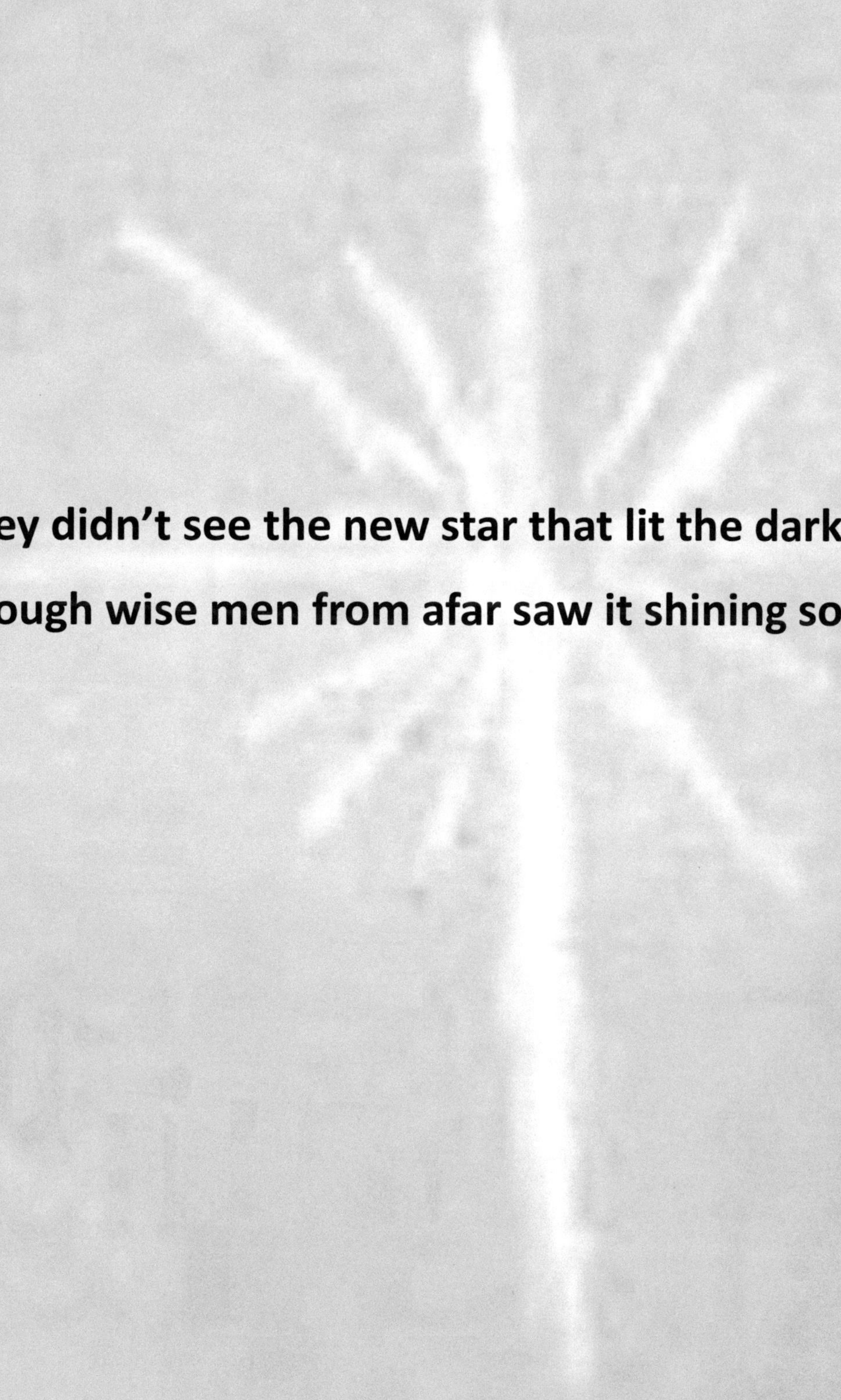

They didn't see the new star that lit the dark night,

Though wise men from afar saw it shining so bright!

The town didn't see the angels nor hear the hosts of them sing;
These people didn't notice — not one single thing!

But the shepherds—they listened and rushed to His side.

They bowed down and worshiped with nothing to hide.

When the shepherds left the stable this beautiful night,

They told the busy townspeople of the miraculous site.

Yet, the people only wondered about what the shepherds said;

They didn't rush to see Jesus nor take a pillow for His head.

And even days later, when to the temple Jesus went,

Only Simeon and Anna were awaiting this event.

JOY
RESTAURANT

Now, are you like the townspeople in this chaotic town,

Too busy with your own plans to notice Jesus is around?

Can you find Him this season with your trees and your presents?

Can you find Him in your Santa?

Your reindeer?

Your pheasants?

PEACE
WOMAN
HOPE
JOY
MEN

Can you find Him in the crowds

shopping for jewelry and toys?

Can you find Him in the faces

of little girls and boys?

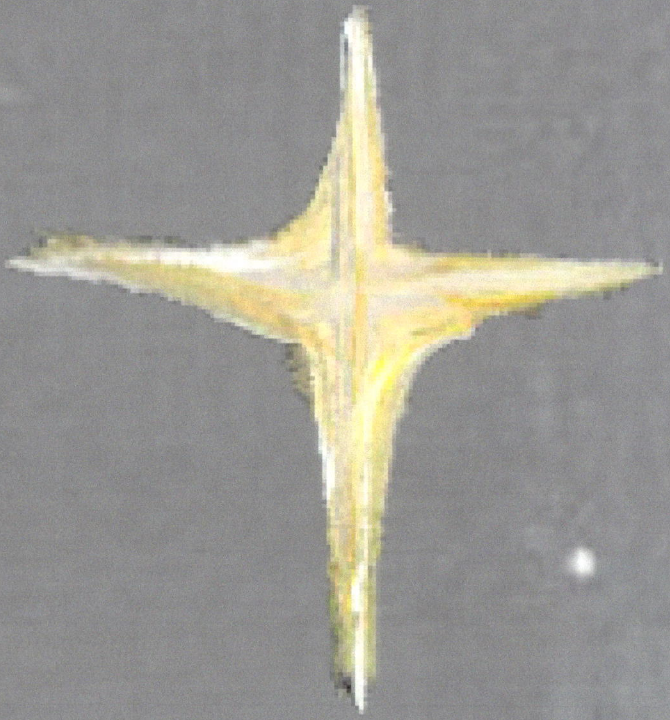

Can you find Him in your parties and productions at church?

You can find Him! You can find Him, if only you'll search!

Don’t be like the townspeople too busy to see;

He’s here in the midst of us!

He’s here — the Prince of Peace!

FOOD

THE STORY BEHIND THE STORY

Some years ago, a particular children's movie was released during the holiday season – one that I desperately wanted to see, and I had almost convinced my husband to go see it with me. However, before we had an opportunity to see it, we stopped by a local retail store which happened to have a huge display featuring toys from this newly released movie. As we approached the display, we overheard a little girl enthusiastically sharing the details of the movie with her inattentive mother. David and I were captivated by the little storyteller and lingered in the area to hear her rendition of this story (We did look at the display, attempting to not appear to be stalkers). The last thing she said, as she drew her arms to her chest was, "It was just so amazing!"

As we walked away, my sweet David said, "Well, now we don't have to see the movie."

To which I responded, "Are you kidding? Now, I wouldn't miss it for the world!"

As we were leaving the parking lot, I replayed the experience in my mind and discussed my impression of the distracted mother. David jumped to the mom's defense, "Think about how many times she has heard that story!" His response settled my concerns. I concluded that she'd become so familiar with the story that she was no longer captivated by it.

Immediately, I heard a still, small voice say, "That's what you've done with My Story."

The Story of Jesus—so many of us have heard it and re-heard it. We've read the book. We've watched pageants and plays and movies about the greatest Story ever told so many times that we are no longer captivated by it. We've become so familiar with the Story and the Storyteller that we've learned to push the ignore button and carry on with our distracted lives, taking care of our personal agendas. Oh, sure, like this mother loves her daughter, we love our Storyteller. We are just busy, so we brush aside the excitement and enthusiasm and no longer let the passion ignite the spark that's in our hearts, just waiting to be ignited so that it can consume us again.

I found myself weary of being complacent and nonchalant about the greatest Story ever told, so I set aside my to-do list, and I allowed myself to be captivated by the Story and the Storyteller again. It has been life-changing.

My prayer is that *Finding Jesus in Christmas* re-ignites the passion of those who know the Story and sparks a new interest in those who may have never heard the Story. As you read and re-read these simple Seussical-style lines, may the Storyteller draw you into the greatest Story ever told. May He be the Peace you are seeking, the Hope that you are needing, and the Everlasting Joy that will quench your soul. May you find opportunities to step away from the chaos, the distractions, the to-do lists, and find Jesus in Christmas once again.

If you seek Him, you will find Him when you seek Him with all of your heart. Jeremiah 29:13

Behold, a virgin shall be with child, and shall bring forth a son, and they shall call his name Emmanuel, which being interpreted is, God with us.

Matthew 1:23

About the Author

VERONICA MARECLE is a principal, teacher, speaker, and writer who enjoys encouraging and inspiring others through the art of storytelling. A lifelong resident of Texas, she dreams of embarking upon new adventures and visiting enchanted places but has discovered those opportunities await her each morning when she opens her front door or steps into her classroom. As a child, Veronica learned the art of putting her pants on two legs at a time because she refused to be like everybody else, and she is convinced that this practice can turn an ordinary day into an extraordinary one. Veronica and her husband, David, spend their free time chasing steeples on long drives in the country and searching for hidden treasures in obscure bookstores where she often gets lost in the pages of a children's storybook.

About the Illustrator

JD DAVENPORT is a native Texas artist whose life experiences are poured into his art. His impressionistic realism style and attention to detail bring his illustrations to life. JD served as a photographer in the U.S. Navy (1987—1992) and engages that knowledge to capture the light in his photographs, paintings, and illustrations. To see more of his work, please visit 3-Joseph-davenport.pixels.com

Made in the USA
Columbia, SC
13 November 2023

26131785R00031